Maximum Employee Engagement: How Healthcare Companies Keep Their Best People

Rhian Sharp (MBA, MHR)

To Elaine
    Thank you for your interest in growing as a leader.
    Your efforts will serve you well as you become more successful in your role.
        all the best
            [signature]
            6/2018

DEDICATION

To my parents for giving me the opportunity to be in this great country, the USA. To my kids for putting up with mommy's long nights of writing, and to the man of my dreams for taking me to the weekend writing class.
Peace and Blessing.

CONTENTS

FOREWARD

Once upon a Joint Commission Visit…

It's 7 am in Atlanta on an unseasonably cool August morning. Tom West, CEO of the facility for over 3 years, has just arrived at his office. As he walks into the building, his Director of Plant Operations, Kathy Cooks, greets him. "Good Morning, Boss!" Kathy exclaims with a warm smile that meets her eyes. "We had a rough night. A couple of beds are offline and three of my staff have called in sick!"

Tom regards Kathy coolly and responds, "What would you like to do?"

Without pausing for breath, Kathy says, "Fire all 3!"

Tom, still cool as ever, says, "Let's discuss during our 1 pm meeting today."

Tom proceeds to make his way to his office. His Executive Assistant, Martha Ray, smiles, says good morning and asks if he would like coffee to start off his day. Tom begins to make himself comfortable, ready to get his day started. As he sits down to check his email, he listens to the sounds of the night shift team clocking out as they leave the facility. There are three voice messages on Tom's phone. One is from his Chief Nursing Officer, Darlene Joseph. Darlene has worked with the facility for over five years. She is a diligent CNO, the perfect mix of clinical expertise and business acumen. Darlene needs to see Tom to discuss the nursing shortage and ends her message with, "Tom, this can't wait, or we will lose more staff… and I may be one of them."

The next message is from the Admissions Director, Frank Wilson. Apparently, Frank too is concerned about his staff. However, Frank's message is short and not as 'sweet' as Darlene's. "Tom," the message from Frank says. "What the heck are we doing?! We only had one person show up last night and had a bunch of referrals that needed processing!" Frank ends his message with, "This staffing situation is costing us census and money!"

The final voice message on his phone is from the front office manager, Leila Watson. Leila seems nervous and concerned. "Um… Mr. West… ah… there's a gentleman here. He's with the Joint Commission."

With that, Tom just about spits out his coffee.

During the last survey, the facility was cited for poor staffing ratios! Tom took action and requested the Human Resources (HR) team work with recruiters to hire new staff members. They were able to hire well over 150 clinical staff in about four weeks, mostly consisting of Registered Nurses (RNs).Unfortunately, only 30 percent of the new hires are still employed and Tom begins to ponder the reason for this. *Why can't we keep our staff? How can we retain our great people?* he thinks.

Is Tom's story familiar to you? Have you hired dozens of great employees only to find that you struggle to keep them for more than a few months or weeks?

As an HR Leader for almost 20 years now, I have seen countless examples of both companies that do an amazing job of keeping great staff and those that seem unable to ever hold onto staff members. What does it take to keep exceptional people? The employer-employee relationship, like all relationships, requires focused effort to ensure maximum commitment over time. For those of us in the healthcare sector, this relationship is made even more complex by the scarcity of people to fill job openings in several healthcare roles. According to the Bureau of Labor Statistics, the unemployment rate in the US has been hovering around four to five percent for the last few years; however, in the healthcare industry, the numbers are closer to two to three percent. When you look at specific jobs such as Child and Adolescent Psychiatrists, the rate is a shocking one percent! These statistics show that we are currently at full employment in the healthcare sector. This makes two simple facts true:

1. Employees that you need to work for you are already employed.
2. Employees currently working for you will go to your competition if you are unable to keep them.

In this book, we will explore the concept of employee engagement, specifically, examining how it is measured. I will also provide you with a step-by-step guide to keeping great employees.

CHAPTER 1:
WHAT IS EMPLOYEE ENGAGEMENT ANYWAY?

I'm sure you have heard the term 'employee engagement' many times before. In recent years, it has become a 'buzz phrase' around many organizations. Your corporate office, HR Director, and external consultants may have communicated to you the importance of high employee engagement, as it directly impacts the facility, your patient satisfaction surveys, your bonus, and your bottom line. If you are a smaller medical office, you may have read articles regarding the benefits of high employee engagement to the continued viability of your practice. But what exactly is employee engagement?

Let me first explain what employee engagement is NOT. Employee engagement is NOT exclusively about tenure. It may be new-aged to say that the topic of tenure is so 1990s, but it is very possible to have a highly tenured employee with low levels of engagement. Let me give you an example. Have you ever visited a facility or medical office run by Nurse Rosemary Rachette? She's been with the facility for 20 years! She is seen as reliable, a decent clinician but with consistently abysmal patient satisfaction surveys, and you may have patients who refuse to visit your office anymore after being cared for by her! In fact, if you do employee option surveys, you may find that a tenured employee, Nurse Rachette in our example, is the main reason you are unable to keep new nurses. These types of employees, while experienced, are not engaged.

HIGH TENURE ≠ MAXIMUM EMPLOYEE ENGAGEMENT

David Macleod, Co-founder of Engaged for Success, offers up the following definition of employee engagement. Mr. Macleod states that employee engagement "is about the conditions in which employees offer more of their capability and potential."

So let's think employee engagement this way….

Employee Engagement: The Dating Analogy

What does it take to have a successful, committed, and highly-evolved romantic relationship? Just being present is not enough, is it? There must be a mutual attraction or 'chemistry,' something to be gained by both people, and feelings of safety, security, and significance. Additionally, both sides must be allowed to continue to grow with a foundation of trust. These environmental factors are crucial for a romantic relationship to thrive. These same environmental factors are important in ensuring the employer-employee relationship is successful as well. When all of these factors line up, you will have a highly engaged team. Employees in an organization where these factors don't line up will only work to earn a paycheck without performing to their maximum potential.

Performance Actualization vs. Earning a Paycheck

Employees who have achieved a high level of engagement have evolved to a level of what I refer to as "Performance Actualization." These employees perform to their maximum potential because they not only have the knowledge, skills, and abilities to do their work but are also working in an environment designed to support their success. An example of this type of employee would be an advance practice nurse, who after being on overnight call, volunteers to help train the daytime admissions team. Why would she do such a thing? Well, the reason for this is that the employee believes in her work and in the company, including its mission and leadership team. She is a valued part of the whole and believes that her individual performance can impact outcomes. This is more than just being a member of a team; it's more like being the team itself. The environment includes not only the necessary technology but also the culture of the company and several other key elements designed for the employee's success.

Maximum Employee Engagement = Knowledge Skills and Abilities + Environment Designed for Success (Including a Culture That Meets Human Needs)

So why do we need more engaged employees? The answer to that is one word: PRODUCTIVITY. Research shows that employees who are more engaged and feel like an integral part of the organization are more productive.

Aimee McKee from the Teleos Leadership Institute says it this way:

"Happy people are better workers. Those who are engaged in their jobs and colleagues work harder and smarter."

In fact, a recent Gallup poll claims companies with high employee engagement scores have a 30 percent higher level of productivity and profitability compared to those with low scores.

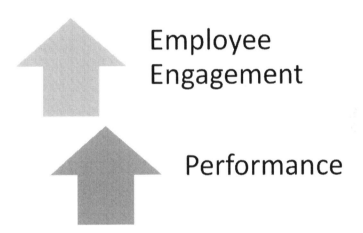

Employee Engagement

Performance

So how do we arrive at maximum employee engagement? Before we look at the steps needed lets first briefly examine how employee engagement is measured.

CHAPTER 2:
HOW TO MEASURE EMPLOYEE ENGAGEMENT

Have you ever heard the phrase, *it's not you, it's me?* Well, today I'm here to tell you that it IS YOU.

The truth is WORK IS PERSONAL. In a recent management survey conducted by Forbes magazine, 56 percent of employees would turn down a 10 percent raise just to stay with a great boss!

How do your employees feel about you? About your hospital or medical office? About the daily work environment? Studies show that human beings tend to be happier and more engaged at work when they feel as if they are a part of the organization and involved in its culture.

People Leave People, Not Companies

Therefore, the tools used to measure levels of employee engagement tend to ask questions not focused on the employee's overall degree of connection to the organization as a whole, but instead specifically about the employee's connection to the people within the organization. I remember working with a healthcare company that paid its business development team very well. The Vice President of Sales, however, was less than approachable. In fact, he was given the not so affectionate name of 'Task Master.' His team had very high turnover rate and, even worse, very low-performance numbers. As a result, the company decided to complete an employee engagement survey using a tool from the company Halogen.

The results of the survey were astonishing to organizational leaders. The Task Master's team had an exceptionally low engagement score in every key indicator listed on the survey. Even though the hospital was meeting the financial needs of the sales team, their other human needs were not being met.

"If you can meet a person's human needs, they will never leave you." - Tony Robbins

What Are These Human Needs?

Psychologists have determined six human needs:

1. Certainty or security
2. Variety and challenge
3. Significance and worth
4. Connection
5. Growth
6. Contribution (going beyond our own needs to give to others)

We now know that highly engaged teams (those that have achieved maximum engagement) perform at higher levels and tend to stay longer at one hospital. It would therefore stand to reason that the hospitals where these teams work are meeting most, if not all, of the employees' human needs.

Employee engagement surveys tend to focus on questions related to these human needs. The following are examples of statements proposed to employees from an actual survey tool.

- I know what is expected of me at work.
- At work, my opinions seem to count.
- I have the materials and equipment I need to do my work right.
- The mission or purpose of my company makes me feel my job is important.
- At work, I have the opportunity to do what I do best every day.
- My associates or fellow employees are committed to doing quality work.
- In the last seven days, I have received recognition or praise for doing good work.
- I have a best friend at work.
- My supervisor, or someone at work, seems to care about me as a person.

- In the last six months, someone at work has talked to me about my progress.
- There is someone at work who encourages my development.
- This last year, I have had opportunities at work to learn and grow.

Now, let's group each of these questions under the specific human need to which they are related.

Certainity	Variety	Significance	Connection	Growth	Contribution
• I know what is expected of me at work • I have the materials and equipment I need to do my work right	• This year I have had opportunities at work to learn and grow	• At work my opinon seems to count • At work I have the opportunity to do what I do best every day • In the last seven days I have recieved recognition or praise for doing good work • My supervisor or someone at work seems to care about me as a person	• My associates or fellow employees are committed to doing quality work • I have a best friend at work	• In the last 6 months somone at work has talked to me about my progress • There is someone at work who encourages my development	• The mission or purpose of the company makes me feel my job is important

CHAPTER 3:

Making the Best Use of the Employee Engagement Survey

Administering the Engagement Survey

Once completed, the employee engagement survey will give you an idea of your employees' perception of how well you meet their needs. I recommend you have an external company administer the survey for the following reasons. Firstly, it's always great to have a specialist for a specialized task (e.g. you wouldn't want an obstetrician doing the work of a cardiologist!). Secondly, it will give your employees the feeling that they can be completely honest when answering. Before you hire an external consulting company to complete the survey, meet with them to ensure you understand how the survey will be administered. Some companies can send the tool to your employees' home emails, while others only send it to work emails. You can work with the external company and decide on what will work best for your facility.

What To Do/Ask When Meeting With the Employee Engagement Survey Consultant

- Ensure that you understand the how to read the survey results. Most employee engagement survey companies will segment the results by company, unit, and individual manager (ex. charge nurse, nursing supervisor, etc.). You should also ask about sample size, as some organizations will share that a too small sample size may not provide valid results. My belief is that as an organizational leader you should ask to see the results for ALL departments, regardless of sample size. This is the only way you can make necessary changes throughout the company.

- Ask the company completing the survey to categorize questions and responses by the aforementioned 'human needs.' They may already have their own way of categorizing, but it will be greatly beneficial to you to have the data categorized in this way. I recommend this to you for the following reasons:
  - o If an organization is satisfying two of an employee's human needs, then the manager or company has a strong connection with the employee.
  - o If the organization is satisfying four of an employee's human needs, then the manager or company has created a bond with the employee.
  - o If the organization is satisfying six of an employee's human needs, then the employee will never want to leave and the organization will have achieved maximum employee engagement.

Review the data carefully; review the results for your overall facility, admission staff, billing office, the director of your nursing team, social services and so on. The idea is to see which teams are highly engaged. Be sure to look out for outliers in the data. Once you have a good grasp of the data, schedule a meeting with all of your managers. This meeting should be a general overview of the results at the organizational level. It is best to review the specific survey data one-on-one with your managers, NOT in the group meeting. Remember your managers also have human needs; you don't want to un-intentionally embarrass someone in a group meeting and hurt their need for significance.

Now that we have learned how to administer the employee engagement survey, categorized the results, reviewed the data, and communicated with our managers, we can turn our attention to the 'main course' of this book. Let's look at the steps we need to take to achieve maximum employee engagement to keep great employees.

****

The Story of Patricia (Lost to a Lengthy Employment Application!)

It's a hot August day in Atlanta, Georgia. I think it must be about 95 degrees with 100 percent humidity. I get a call from an old colleague, Laura. She has taken on the new CEO role with a very reputable company in Virginia. "How the heck are you?" Laura asks, beaming over the phone.

"Great!" I beam back. "How the heck are you?" I'm all smiles. Laura begins sharing that she loves her new behavioral health hospital. They have great referral sources, a new set of buildings, and great psychiatrists on staff. She shares that her biggest challenge has been finding and keeping great RNs.

"I sure could use your help," she sighs, but I know she's still beaming with excitement over her new gig.

"I'd be happy to help!" I exclaim. "I'll send over a staffing agreement to your HR team today and work to get you some wonderful RNs ASAP!"

As we end the call, I'm super excited. I begin looking up information on the facility online and looking at the employee and patient feedback on Glassdoor and other sites. Hmmmm… the comments on Glassdoor are concerning. The facility rating is a 1.5 out of 5! It appears that a lot of the adverse comments are due to shortages of staff and the resulting frustration and exhaustion felt by existing staff. I am, however, not deterred by the negative comments. I press on, emailing the contract and beginning my search for the perfect psychiatric RNs.

In less than three days, I have seven candidates pre-screened and ready for interviews with the Director of Nursing (DON) and her team. I call Laura to share the good news. She's ecstatic but shares that we should get the candidates through to HR because the application process takes YEARS to get through.

Patricia was one of the first psych RNs I screened. She had previously heard about the facility, had several years of both inpatient and outpatient behavioral health experience, and was excited about the opportunity to work for the facility. Per Laura's request, I email Patricia's resume and my notes to the HR team. Two days pass and I still have not received feedback. I call the HR Director, Sean. "Hi, Sean. Have you been able to review the resumes of the RN candidates?" I ask, hopefully.

"I sure have," Sean responds, sounding exhausted. "I've just been so busy… I didn't have time to respond to you."

"Not a problem," I respond, trying to sound encouraging. "Let's see if we can get her scheduled for an interview. She did have a Skype call with your DON and the team loved her, so I don't want you guys to lose her."

"I see," he says, sounding upset. "Well, we need her to complete an application, drug testing, a personality survey, and a few other things," he says smartly. "Can you send her the application link?" he asks hopefully.

"Sure! I'll do so now." As soon as I hang up the phone I call Patricia. She promises to complete the application ASAP. The next day I get a call from Patricia around noon.

"Hey, Ms. Sharp... did you know the application is 119 pages long?!" Patricia says sounding both shocked and disappointed.

"Really!?' I respond, legitimately surprised.

"I worked a twelve-hour shift last night... I'm super tired and won't be able to get to this application finished today... I can do it over the weekend." I share with Patricia that I completely understand and will check in with her on Monday to see how the application process is going.

On Sunday evening I get a call at around 7pm from Patricia. "I'm sorry to call you on a Sunday, Ms. Sharp, but my current employer found out that I was job hunting and gave me a big bump in pay."

"Wow!" I respond. "Would you be open to continuing the process with Laura's company?" I ask praying for a positive response.

"No... to be honest, Ms. Sharp, the company seems very disorganized and that application was the worst thing I have seen in all my years of nursing!"

I must share that Patricia's experience was not an isolated one. Of the seven RNs we found, only one was able to complete the application process without receiving a counteroffer from their current employer.

DON'T LET YOUR PROCESSES LOSE YOU GREAT PEOPLE!

****

CHAPTER 4:
The 6 Steps to Maximum Employee Engagement

Now that your company has completed the employee engagement survey, you can begin to make meaningful changes to ensure ALL your teams have the steps needed to ensure maximum employee engagement.

During my 20 years as an HR Executive in the healthcare field, both in the US and abroad, I have observed that companies that work diligently on the following steps tend to have maximum employee engagement.

The following six steps also align directly with your employee's human needs and create an engaging organizational culture that will lead to maximum employee engagement.

1. Ensure a great talent acquisition and recruiting experience
2. Provide an unforgettable onboarding experience
3. Offer competitive compensation and an employee benefits plan
4. Develop meaningful training
5. Engage in truly collaborative performance reviews
6. Create transparent succession planning

Why is Creating an Engaging Culture Important?

Think of it this way: remember when you were dating and trying to find that perfect man or woman? One of the first steps psychologists recommend is to take some time to really discover who you are, what you stand for, what are your likes and dislikes are, and who are the people you want to attract. It is important to be your genuine self, but even more important to be the best version of your genuine self.

Similarly, before you can attract people who will be maximally engaged with your facility, you need to be clear and honest about your organization's culture. As a leader, it is important to ask yourself the questions below. Write your answers to these questions on paper. Be honest about your company's unique culture. Don't consider the cultures you've witnessed at other companies or other hospitals.

- What are your organizational beliefs?
- What are your core values?
- Which non-profits do you support?
- What are your mission and vision?
- Do your managers understand your mission, vision, and values? How do you know?
- Do your managers believe in your mission, vision, and values? How do you know?

- Do your managers share the mission, vision, and values with employees? How do you know?
- What is your corporate brand in the marketplace?

Once you have answered all the questions above be use your answers to formulate a mission statement, something that is simple and other managers can utilize as a consistent message to share with employees. This statement will be a verbal representation of your organizational culture.

Here is an example of a simple and yet powerful mission statement from the Patagonia company:

"Build the best product, cause no unnecessary harm, and use business to inspire and implement solutions to the environmental crisis."

Now that you have started creating a genuine and engaging corporate culture, you need to take a look at your corporate brand. How powerful is your company's brand? What do employees think of your brand compared to other employers?

Let's look at what's needed to ensure your corporate brand is strong enough to attract the right people to your hospital or medical office.

Steps to Creating a Powerful Corporate Brand

- Audit your online presence
- Polish your company website
- Find ways to produce valuable content
- Be purposeful about what you share
- Associate with other powerful brands

It is important to note the maximum employee engagement occurs long before new employees join your organization. It begins when the people you want to attract and retain start to follow your brand. Thus, you must not only build the power of your brand but also the 'street credibility' of your company. Pay close attention to comments made on online platforms such as Glassdoor. These ratings and comments can significantly impact your chances of attracting the right people to your organization.

Audit Your Organization's Online Presence

When was the last time you did a Google search of your company's name? If you are the leader of the organization or in a leadership role when was the last time you did a Google search of your own name? It is crucial to stay on top of what is being said about your brand in the cyber world. Ratings and comments can significantly impact your ability to attract good employees to your company.

As a headhunter, I can tell you that candidates ARE looking at your organization's online persona. The ratings and comments on Glassdoor, for example, are particularly powerful. I have had several highly qualified candidates turn down the opportunity to interview with an organization because of poor ratings on Glassdoor. So being diligent about what is said about your organization is of paramount importance.

If possible, ask employees who have had positive experiences with your organization to go online and rate and/or comment. This will help improve your organization's overall rating over time on online platforms like Glassdoor.

Polishing and Updating Your Company Website

Your company website is the organizational version of a resume. At a glance, it must inform the viewer about your organization, and give them a sense of your mission, vision, and values. It must communicate the atmosphere you want to convey to potential customers and employees.

Do you have a careers page on your website? What images or messages does it convey about your company and its culture?

For potential new employees, a careers page is a great window into your company's world. The more vibrant and current your careers page, the greater the likelihood you will attract the right potential candidates. The careers page should be targeted to specific types of candidates you hope to attract. Are you hoping to attract Generation Xs or Millennials? Are your best employees ones who attended a specific college or program? Do they have families? What are their core needs? Consider these questions and more when designing your careers page.

BE CREATIVE, GENUINE, AND UNIQUE, AND THINK OF

SOME CATCHY TAGLINES AS WELL

The table below communicates great examples of how specific generational groups prefer to receive information. Research holds that these are the common traits of each generational group. However, please remember that everyone is an individual with unique needs.

Our four generation workforce provides challenges

Seniors	Baby Boomers	Gen Xers	Gen Yers
b. 1920-1945	b. 1946-1965	b. 1966-1979	b. 1980-2000

Note: Be sure that your marketing strategy around creating a career page holds up to legal compliance. Remember that it is illegal to discriminate based on Title VII. Be sure to talk with a legal profession.

Find Ways to Produce Valuable Content

The best way to communicate your mission, vision, and values (i.e. your company brand) is to find ways of packaging your brand in the form valuable content. Large companies have communications directors and staff to help with brand awareness and media plugs, but small companies can do this as well. Here are a few ideas to get started:

- **Utilize Help A Reporter** (www.haro.com). This site connects reporters looking for stories to people who can provide content. It's a great way to get positive media exposure for you, your managers, and your organization.

- **Think about starting a CEO blog** focused on your brand what is important to your employees and the candidates you are trying to attract. For example, if most of your employees are interested in providing shelter for the homeless, talk about how much your company gives to homeless shelters or how your employees visit the shelters every month to provide food and clothing.

- **Utilize Linked In.** Linked In is in essence Facebook for business. On Linked In, you will be communicating directly with potential employees. Be sure your content is targeted to what's trending and of importance to your target audience. For example, with the prevalence of sexual harassment claims, discuss how your company works to ensure zero tolerance for sexual harassment.

- **Create employer videos on YouTube.** People love watching videos. Research shows that an effective video is more likely to have a lasting impact than a written post. Try doing a weekly or monthly YouTube video talking about the great things happening at your company. Invite various managers to participate in these videos with you.

- **Record a podcast.** In a recent Forbes article, it was reported that over 112 million Americans listen to podcasts! This medium of communication continues to be very popular and is another great way to communicate your brand to your target market.

- **Send out e-newsletters.** Most organizations have a newsletter they share with employees and vendors. It's also a great idea to create an e-newsletter to be shared on your website, company Facebook page, Linked In and more.

Be Purposeful About What You Share

Take a look at how things work in Hollywood or the world of politics! Do you think all of those Tweets are by accident?! The truth is there is usually a specific purpose behind what is communicated in the press. You need to treat your messages the same way. Define your purpose and communicate your message in the right medium for your business. Your goal is to achieve Maximum Employee Engagement, so the messages you share should focus on how your company is meeting the human needs of its employees.

Sharing employee testimonials are great! PR company Cision communicated recently that 70% of Millennials are influenced by the recommendations of their peers.

Associate With Other Powerful Brands

In marketing, this technique is called co-branding. The key to making this work for your organization and brand is being sure the brand you are partnering with has a similar mission, vision, and value to your company's and that your target audience (in this case employees and potential employees) believe in the brand you are partnering with. Take, for example, Coca-Cola and McDonald's. These two brands have been growing together since 1955! Both brands have power and can attract employees and consumers, which is enhanced through messages from both brands.

CHAPTER 5:
A Great Talent Acquisition and Recruiting Experience

So now that you have created a powerful corporate brand to attract the right people, it's time to 'sell' that brand to your candidates. The reason I'm using the term 'sell' is that with unemployment at 4 percent and in the healthcare industry at 2 percent, it is critical that employers work diligently to find the best people. As I shared early in this book, low unemployment numbers mean that many of your potential candidates are already employed. Employers in the healthcare sector need to be aggressive about acquiring talent.

It is important that your entire talent acquisition and recruiting process be a pleasant experience for your candidates. If I had a dollar for every time candidates shared with me that the recruiting process was too long or complicated, I would be super rich!

It is important to take the following steps related to the recruiting process:

- **Hire dynamic, attractive, and professional recruiters**. I know what you're thinking... yes, being attractive is important. Jim Rohn said that to attract you have to be attractive. I don't mean this in the provocative spokes model sense. What I mean is that you need to be sure that you have recruiters and recruiting partners who share your company vision. They need to be diligent about actively reaching out the candidates, they should be accomplished 'cold callers,' and they need to be great at follow up. In a nutshell, your recruiters need to be salespeople.

- **Your recruiters must have a sense of urgency**. The need to understand that the worst word in the English language, worse than the infamous 'f' word, is 'tomorrow.' You need to reach candidates before your competitors do, and even if you talk with someone who is not a fit, be sure to follow up and stay in touch with them. Of the thousands of new employees that stayed with my organizations over the years, over 90 percent communicated that they joined the company because of how much they liked their interaction with the recruiter or headhunter. Don't discount this connection.

- **Make your employment application quick, easy, and accessible**. We've all seen them: employment applications that are the length of your mortgage paperwork or an edition of War and Peace! I often ask my clients about their application process. Think about it: this is one of the first experiences a candidate will have with your organization. Do you want to give the impression that your company is a complex and rigid organization? Don't you want your candidates to join with the understanding that you make things simple to achieve your ultimate goals? Remember that in today's unemployment market, your potential employees are likely already working for other employers. If they work in healthcare settings, they may be working the night shift or have been held over to work a double shift if their hospital is short staffed. They really don't have the time, energy, or patience to complete a lengthy application. My recommendation is to have your candidate only complete the basic items needed to get them through the screening process. Then streamline the remainder of your application. Make sure it's accessible on mobile devices. Non-critical items should be completed once your offer letter has been signed. Once the offer is extended and signed, you are on your way to maximum employee engagement. The candidate has decided to join. Having someone complete piles of paperwork before they have even agreed to join your team is like asking someone to move in with you on the first date! Save the paperwork for the onboarding process.

- **Ensure an outstanding interview experience**. When I talk to candidates I have submitted to my client. I always ask them how they 'enjoyed' the interview. I use the word enjoyed purposefully. I want them to have enjoyed the experience of meeting with the hiring manager and learning about their prospective company. I want them to feel as if they belong in the culture communicated during the interview. Remember how we discussed earlier in this book that people tend to stay with employers who fulfill their basic human needs? So, if an interview fulfills a candidate's need for belonging and acceptance, then they will not only join the organization, but will also they have a high potential to be maximally engaged once on-board.

What makes a great interview experience? After talking with thousands of candidates over the last 20 years, I have compiled the following list of the top ten things shared by candidates:

1) The facility's or office had a nice appearance
2) The front office was friendly and greeted them
3) The front office was expecting them and knew their name
4) Everyone seemed to be smiling
5) The hiring manager was on time for the interview
6) The hiring manager seemed nice (smiling, pleasant, friendly, and approachable)
7) The hiring manager seemed knowledgeable
8) The candidate learned a lot of about the good the company does for customers and employees
9) The company took the time to show the candidate around
10) The hiring manager seemed to like the candidate and thought he or she would be a good fit

As you can see from the list above, these points are all about how the interview made the candidate feel!

Questions That Make for More Enjoyable Interviews

Adaptability
Change is inevitable in any workplace, so it's no surprise that adaptability is the top soft skill hiring managers look for. Their favorite questions to screen for adaptability are:

1. Tell me about a time when you were asked to do something you had never done before.
2. Describe a situation in which you embraced a new system, process, technology, or idea at work that was a major departure from the old way of doing things.

Culture Fit
Employees who mesh well with a company's culture are more likely to be productive and stick around, so hiring managers will look for alignment between your values and the company's. The most popular culture-fit questions are:

1. What are the three things that are most important to you in a job?
2. Tell me about a time in the last week when you've been satisfied, energized, and productive at work. What were you doing?

Collaboration

Almost every job on the planet involves working with others, so having one or two teamwork examples up your sleeve is critical. Here are hiring managers' leading questions for discerning collaboration skills:

1. Give an example of when you had to work with someone who was difficult to get along with.
2. Tell me about one of your favorite experiences working with a team and your contribution.

CHAPTER 6:
Orientation and Onboarding and the Plan

Employees' first few days with your organization are critical. Most HR experts agree that the most important formative days are from day one to day ninety.

Onboarding occurs during the first 90 days of employment. At this time the new hire is still unsure of the new job and is still reeling from the interview phase. If they haggled a bit over the offer letter, they may be feeling a bit self-conscious about asking for more money or benefits. In addition, this is also your opportunity to see how well the new hire fits into your organizational culture. The first 90 days are the equivalent of the honeymoon phase of a relationship. This employment phase is referred to as the onboarding phase. During this phase, the new hire will be indoctrinated to the culture of your organization, its mission, and values.

Orientations occurred during the first few days of employment. In healthcare, organizations tend to have a 3 to 5-day long orientation for new hires. This is due in part the compliance requirements and to the complexity of some large hospital systems. It is very important the during the orientation and onboarding phase new hires feel valued, significant, welcomed and a part of the culture.

THE FIRST 90 DAYS OF EMPLOYMENT IS THE EQUIVALENT OF THE HONEYMOON PHASE OF A RELATIONSHIP

Power of the Peer Mentor

Before the employee starts work, consider partnering them with another employee, a peer mentor, for their first 30 days. Remember one of the key questions from the employee engagement survey: "I have a best friend at work." Studies show that people who form close personal bonds at work have a lower percentage of absenteeism, are more productive, and are more engaged. This is especially important in high-stress environments such as healthcare facilities. I recommend that you choose peer mentors that meet the following qualifications:

- They are good performers
- They are positive role models of the company's culture (i.e. the model your company's mission, vision, and values)
- They have similar interests to the new hire

The peer mentor can be given a small stipend for lunch or coffee with the new hire. Additionally, it's even better for the peer mentor to welcome the new hire with a call or email before the day of orientation. Of course, you should have your HR Director, Communications Manager, or Office Manager create a standard welcome to be sent by the mentor. This simple act can go a long way towards maximizing employee engagement in your newly hired employees.

Now Let me share with you a simple 3-step process that I have utilized with my clients. These simple steps will make your orientations stand out to your new hires.

Three Steps to Outstanding Orientations

Step 1: Setting the Stage

The location of the orientation meeting is important. First of all, the room should be easy for the new employee to find. I have spoken with new hires I placed in hospitals who spent hours trying to locate the meeting room. Remember that even though the new hire has signed your offer letter, they are still in the process of confirming their decision to join. They are nervous and anxious, so make it easy for them from the start.

I advise my clients to place a welcome sign in their lobby area on orientation day. List the names of the new employees joining; most people like to see their names and enjoy the feeling of being welcomed. It is one of the human needs we discussed earlier in the book.

In most organizations, orientation begins in the morning. In healthcare organizations, due to the volume of documents needed for regulatory compliance, most orientations can last for about five days. I would strongly recommend companies provide refreshments for their new hires, as human beings tend to bond over a meal. In addition, this adds to the feeling of being welcomed and belonging.

Step 2: Have All Documents Ready, Along With Give-A-Ways

We know that there is always paperwork new employees are required to complete. However, it is possible to add a bit of fun to the process. If possible, email or text new hires a link where they can complete their documents online. However, even if you have emailed all of your new hires, ALWAYS have a neat new hire package available on the day of your orientation meeting. The package should be placed in a folder with your company logo. Consider other useful items that display your organization brand as well. Pens, pencils, coffee mugs, hand sanitizer, and candy are just a few examples of small items you can give out.

Create an individualized 90-day plan and let the employees know that their hiring manger created the plan to ensure their successful start with the company. Be sure to make it clear that the employee's manager is invested in their success. By saying this, you are again catering to the employee's need for significance and belonging.

You can visit www.sharpmedicalrecruiting.com/forms, where you will find an example of an actual 90-day plan utilized by one my clients. The template of the plan is the standard, however, each hiring manager should make small adjustments based on what he or she learned about the new hire during the interview phase. For example, let's say that during week two of the new hire's training, they have to learn to enter data into an electronic medical record (EMR). During the interview, you may have discovered that the new hire used paper records in previous positions. Given this information, you should tweak the time needed for training regarding this specific topic for this individual.

Step 3: Be Visible

We've learned that work is personal and that people join or leave organizations because of human connections or lack thereof. Employees will be engaged and stay with organizations when their human needs are being met. So, it is important that leaders attend some portion of the employee orientation. I advise my clients that the CEO should be present on day one. The CEO needs to set the tone as he or she will be the face of the company and must communicate the vision, mission, and values. Join the new hire for breakfast or lunch. Be approachable and ask them questions. Allow them an opportunity to get to know you on a personal level. Remember to be purposeful about what you share. For example, new employees love to learn about growth opportunities. Talk with them about your journey, how you worked your way up to your current position.

Each member of the leadership team should visit with the new hires to share a bit about themselves, their team, and how each division connects to the whole. Organizational charts are helpful but talking with the new hire about the organizational structure in a fun way that includes them will help them remember. For example, in a hospital setting, the admissions director may talk about the process and referrals. Then the utilization review director can talk about the discharge planning process and show how the two teams work together from entry to exit of the facility. Again, if each leader could join the new hires for breakfast or lunch that will go a long will to establishing trust. Once your orientation is complete, I recommend each new hire's manager take them to their workstation.

   NOTE: If you don't have a formal group orientation you can still follow the same process for an individual new hire. Set the stage with a welcome note at the lobby. Be on time to welcome them to the team and to their new unit. Take the time to have lunch with them. Have them meet with different leaders in the organization throughout the day, including the CEO. Finally, be sure to meet with them to review their individualized 90-day plan.

CHAPTER 7:

Competitive Compensation and Benefits Plans

So, let's face it… people join companies to get paid. Yes, it's true that in healthcare and other industries employees have a 'calling' to be an RN or physician. However, we all have bills to pay! While I do believe that money is not everything when it comes to maximizing employee engagement, it is a very significant factor.

Salary is a tricky thing when it comes to employee retention and engagement. It's not about how much you are paying your employees, but rather about how much you are paying relative to what employees in similar roles in other organizations are making. It is important to know how your salaries match up in the marketplace. Are you paying your nurses more than, less than, or on par with other hospitals? If you are not the highest payer in the marketplace, think about what you can offer to offset the pay gap. For example, do you offer set schedules or do your nurses get called in on the weekend? Do you offer an online or automated scheduling system? What about paid time off?

There are several companies that conduct salary studies in the form of surveys so you can obtain information on how your wages compare to those of other organizations in your industry. In fact, you can visit the Department of Labor online via the Bureau of Labor Statistics (www.bls.gov) and obtain some basic salary information.

Screenshot from the actual BLS.gov site:

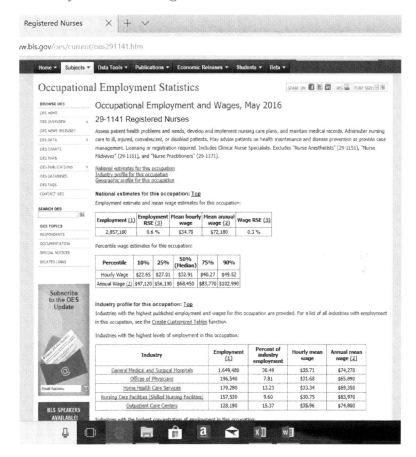

As I have shared with my clients, compensation is made up of two parts:

1. Hard compensation: salary, bonus pay, and incentive pay (i.e. dollars)
2. Soft compensation: paid time off, set schedules, no weekend call, medical benefits, and Employee Assistance Program (i.e. EAP)

If your 'hard compensation' is less than market rates then your goal is to increase awareness of your 'soft compensation' programs. This way, employees will not feel that they are not being paid fairly for their work, which could decrease their feeling of significance. This, in turn, would cause them to be less or not at all engaged in your organization. So, if you are unable to complete with base pay, be sure to really market your soft compensation. For example, talk about how much your people love the 50 percent discount on Care.com or how they appreciate the fact that your company has an annual bring your kids to work party or free coffee in the break rooms. Create posters and videos with employees talking about these soft compensation benefits.

Go to www.SharpMedicalRecruiting.com/MEE for a list of "soft compensation ideas.

Merit Review and Compensation Plans

I believe that most companies don't do a great job when it comes to employee merit reviews. HR leaders have a plethora of online tools available to make the merit process automated and streamlined. We are now able to track the entire performance review process, from form creation to the rating received. So why is it that our merit reviews don't work to maximize employee engagement? Remember that maximizing employee engagement is about satisfying an employee's personal needs. My experience as an HR leader working with thousands of employees over the last 20 years is that the annual merit review is not an effective tool. It fails to really convey how an individual's performance matters and how it makes a difference to the organization as a whole. For the merit process to be effective, I recommend taking the following steps:

1) Create a compensation plan with milestones
2) Communicate how the individual's performance makes a difference to the organization
3) Demonstrate the financial reward of this performance

Most HR Leaders do not like to administer the merit and compensation reviews at the same time. However, my experience with thousands of employees has demonstrated that employees expect compensation and performance to connect. Employees want to see the significance of their work and the resulting pay. After all, this is the primary reason we work.

The Performance/Compensation plans can look something like this example below:

Goal	Target (Expectation)
Infection Control/Safety and Emergency skills	100%
Meals and Feeding	95%
Personal Care Skills	98%
Elimination Skills	95%
Vital Sign Skills	100%
Positioning Skills	95%
Ambulation Skills	95%

Milestone	Rating (1-5 with 5 being the highest)	Possible Increase Highest possible 5% of base	Recommendations for improvement	Feedback from Employee
30 days	2	1%	Work with team lead on personal care skills.	Bi-weekly follow up requested
60 days	3	2.5%	Great improvement in personal care. Will work with Supervisor on Ambulation	Bi-weekly follow up to continue
90 days	3.5	3%	Improvement still needed in Ambulation. Trending towards an end of year increase of 3%	Monthly follow up requested

For your own FREE copy of these charts, go to:
www.SharpMedicalRecruiting.com/MEE

Please note that the example of above shows not only the current performance at each milestone but also shows how the employee is trending towards their possible increase. Finally, it offers recommendations on how to improve to get to this maximum level.

This approach reinforces the fact that you are invested in the employee's success. It allows for ongoing communication, and best of all, if communicated frequently it will prevent performance surprises that could result in adverse performance discussions.

CHAPTER 8:
Meaningful Training

Do you remember that scene from *Ferris Bueller's Day Off*? The teacher stands at the front of the class, checking off names and repeating in a monotone voice, "Bueller, Bueller, Bueller." Don't let this happen to your training program!

Training should be dynamic, impactful, and lasting. In most healthcare organizations in the United States, there is mandatory annual training that must be completed. It becomes a 'check the boxes' exercise, which is unfortunate, as training our employees in a meaningful way can be a significant way to maximize employee engagement.

So how can we develop more meaningful training? First of all, we need to change the way we think about providing our employees with new skills. In the past, I have heard leaders say things like, "Why would I train my healthcare technician in management skills?" if I do that, they'll want to leave and get another job, or they'll ask for more money!" This is NOT the right way to look at training.

Meaningful training happens when the following criteria are met:

- You understand your employee's knowledge, skills, and abilities
- You identify whether those KSAs are being fully utilized in the employee's current role.
- You identify the 'hidden' skills the employee has that have not been utilized in their current role.
- You understand what really motivates your employee.

Many employees experience what I refer to as *Career Dissonance*.

Career Dissonance occurs when you are working in a job that you are qualified for, but is not your innate passion. Career Dissonance never leads to employee engagement, and instead leads to a lack of motivation, low productivity, and burn out. All of us have varying degrees of career dissonance. For example, there are days when I would like to focus on weight training and running but I need to call my next candidates! Weight training and running are my passions. It is important for me to entertain my passions so that I don't experience burnout in my profession. Therefore managers can minimize the impact of career dissonance through training. If you train your employees towards their passion as well as the training that needs to be accomplished for the sake of compliance, you will diminish Career Dissonance in your people.

So, for example, let's say you have a Child and Adolescent Psychiatrist in your facility. She has expressed to you that while she is well versed in the uses of Suboxone, she feels a passion for utilizing exercise, diet, and other integrative approaches in her work as well. The training for this employee should therefore include the necessary annual training as well as annual training in integrative medicine. You may even decide to send her to an integrative medicine seminar. In this example, your employee may not be able to use integrative approaches in your facility, but she may be able to do so at another facility. This is not a problem or a concern. You should only be concerned with keeping her interested to maximize her engagement. You are keeping her focused and satisfied and the work is meeting her human needs.

CAREER DISSONANCE OCCURS WHEN AN EMPLOYEE'S JOB DOES NOT MATCH THEIR PASSION

CHAPTER 9:
Truly Collaborative Performance Reviews

Over the last 20 years, the performance review process has become streamlined and automated. I remember the days of having to create annual reviews forms by hand! Today companies such as Success Factors have created online tools to allow managers to create online review forms, track the completion of review documents, and review ratings in order to calibrate results by department. All this technology is wonderful! However, many of the managers that I have worked with still dreaded the annual merit review. In addition, employees view annual reviews akin to going to the principal's office! So, a process that can be very beneficial in keeping employees engaged often misses the mark! How can we make the performance review process more collaborative and meaningful?

Steps to making the annual merit review process more effective:

- **Show employees how their performance impacts the organization.** As I mentioned before, we all need to belong and be significant. It may be easier for a nurse to see how her performance directly impacts the hospital's overall patient satisfaction, but it may be more difficult for the HR Coordinator to see the connection. It is, however, very important for all employees to see how they impact the big picture. In the case of the HR Coordinator of a hospital, you could show how ensuring employee files are well-maintained leads to better survey scores, allowing the hospital to stay open and provide service to patients.

- **Don't make the annual review a surprise**. Performance management should be an ongoing part of being a manager, as it's a fundamental role of a leader. The annual review should only be the culmination of many performance discussions that have occurred throughout the year. Over the years, I have seen managers who say "Great work" to the employee throughout the year and then at the annual review time inform them that they are not performing to the organization's expectations. Granted, it is very hard for some managers to deal with conflict. Conflict happens and we need to be comfortable with conflict. If an employee is doing well on their targets, let them know. If they are not, let them know that as well. The key is to create a schedule throughout the year to sit with your employees and review how they are performing.

- **Get your employee's feedback**. Talking about job performance should not be a one-sided event. Many of the automated performance management tools start the process by giving employees an option to rate their own performance. This is a great way to maximize engagement as it shows that you value their thoughts and ideas. The challenge is remembering to ask for feedback from employees each time we have a discussion about their performance. We need to understand if the employee is having challenges with a specific goal and whether they have the tools to do their jobs or if they need additional training. We need to continue to show that we are invested in the employee's success. High level of commitment from a manager will help maximize employee engagement.

A Few Thoughts on Performance Corrections

Over the years, I've shared the following phrase with my clients: 'no one starts a job wanting to do poorly.' Everyone starts a new job with hopes of doing well. However, we all know that not everyone is cut out to succeed in every position. As much as we may work to be sure that we achieve 100 percent maximum engagement, we know that not all employees will be strong performers.

It is important to remember that even if an employee is not performing to company expectations, managers are still required to uphold the company brand and culture. Don't ever let a performance discussion or termination lead to uncordial behavior that ends up being communicated on Glassdoor or Facebook! The rest of your employees and their network are looking at you. The three main rules for any challenging discussion such as terminations are to:

- Document in a timely manner
- Don't put off the discussion and instead address the situation quickly
- Be respectful by keeping your emotions in check (this includes your body language and voice inflection)

****

A Messy Termination (Based on a True Story)

Kathy has been psychiatric a nurse practitioner at her hospital for four years. Her immediate manager, Dr. Charles, saw Kathy as a sound clinician, but she was concerned about Kathy's attendance and incident reporting. When conflicts between patients occurred in Kathy's presence, she would walk away, saying, "That's the job of the Nurse Manager... it's not my job."

Mr. Frank, the hospital's CEO, continuously received complaints from the team about Kathy's absence or lack of cooperation during violent incidents with patients.

One December evening, a psychotic patient began to lash out at staff members and other patients in the unit. Kathy was present during this event. The RNs and mental health technicians worked diligently to stabilize the patient. The Nurse Case Manager called out for Kathy's help, but Kathy responded, "Girl, you got that under control," and left the scene!

The next morning, the Nurse Manager visited Mr. Frank to complain about Kathy's behavior. "I've had it with her!" The nurse manager exclaimed. "This has been happening for too long! Someone must do something about Kathy or we will lose more staff!"

After visiting with the Nurse Manager, Mr. Frank went to visit with Dr. Charles. "Doc... we must do something about Kathy," Mr. Frank lamented. "The team has lost all respect for her and she is now losing credibility with us as well." Mr. Frank furrows his brow as he looks at Dr. Charles. "Did you give a verbal or written warning after the last incident?"

Dr. Charles lowers her eyes to her desk and without looking up again says,

"No… I never got around to that."

Mr. Frank, taking a deep breath, says to Dr. Charles, "Please talk with her today."

At 5:30 pm, Dr. Charles asks the front desk to page Kathy to her office. At 6:30 pm Kathy arrives. "What seems to be the problem, Doctor?" asks Kathy.

"Well… it's not really anything major, Kathy," Dr. Charles stumbles. "It's just that… well… the staff has complained about you to Mr. Frank." Dr. Charles goes on to say, "And they want me to have a talk with you."

Kathy inhales sharply and says in a louder voice, "What's the complaint about?!"

Dr. Charles responds, "Please calm down, Kathy. It's just a matter of cooperation. The team is feeling as though you don't support them."

Kathy responds, "Don't tell me to calm down. Those incidents are not my responsibility!"

Dr. Charles responds, "Well they are… you are part of the team and I've been asked by Mr. Frank to write you up!"

Kathy responds in a much louder voice, "You're writing me up! I have worked my ass off and you are writing me up! "Kathy then storms out of Dr. Charles's office and goes straight to Mr. Frank. Upon walking into Mr. Frank's office, Kathy takes off her badge, places it on Mr. Frank's desk, and says, "I QUIT!"

****

So, what went wrong? What would you have done differently? How could this have all been prevented?

Always remember that difficult discussions, for example talking to someone about their poor performance or attendance, or having to tell someone that you have decided to end their employment, require a great deal of tact. It is important to empathize with the employee. You may not agree with the way they have behaved, but you need them to leave your organization knowing you treated them fairly and with respect. Be mindful of the words you use, your body language, and your energy level at the time of the day you choose to have the meeting. Be at your best so that you can make a difficult discussion easier for the employee and company.

CHAPTER 10:
Transparent Succession Planning

Several years ago, I worked with a large healthcare organization that did an amazing job of hiring the right employees, processing merit reviews expeditiously, and administering compensation strategies with the utmost precision. The organization also had a very robust succession planning process. However, despite all these great tools, there was one problem. The company's top performers kept leaving! The company kept losing its best employees because of one issue: they did not communicate to their top performers that they were considered High Potential employees who could eventually move into key organizational roles.

So, what exactly is Succession Planning and why is it important in ensuring maximum employee engagement?

Succession planning is defined as the process of identifying and developing internal employees with the potential to fill key business leadership positions in the company. It is a way for companies to increase the number of experienced and capable employees that are prepared to assume these key roles as they become available. Thus, succession planning is an active way of showing employees that the company is actively creating a culture focused on their growth. Developing and promoting talent from within the organization sends a positive message to employees about the organization's investment in their success.

STEPS OF SUCCESSION PLANNING:

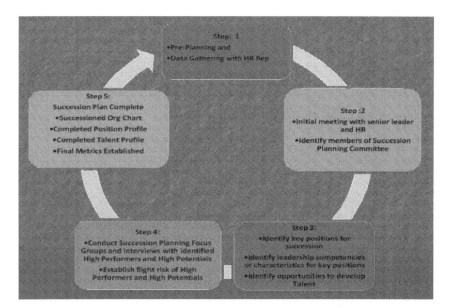

Most organizations develop a Succession Planning process similar to the plan depicted in the above diagram. We won't go into too much detail about the process itself, but the main thing we need to focus on is the goal of a succession plan and how it leads to maximum employee engagement.

The succession planning process is focused on gathering as much information about an organization's high potential (HI-PO) employees as possible. Companies utilize data from the employee's personnel files, feedback from patient and customer surveys, sales surveys, and 360 reviews (i.e. where peers and supervisors are asked for feedback about the employee) to determine which employees have high potential.

In many large organizations, personality assessments are conducted. An example of an in-depth personality assessment is the Predictive Index (PI). I've shared an example of a PI that I completed a few years ago. As you can see, the data points are very in-depth.

MY ACTUAL PREDICTIVE INDEX RESULTS

Predictive Index® Results

Rhian Sharp
Survey Date: 12/20/2013
Report Date: 12/22/2013

Note: A = level of Dominance

B = Level of Extroversion

C = Level of Patience

D = Level of Formality

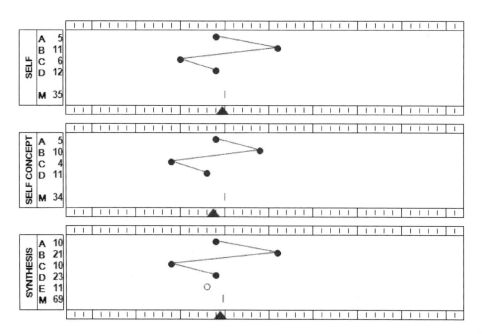

PI for: Rhian Sharp Date: 12/20/2013

The results of the Predictive Index® survey should always be reviewed by a trained Predictive Index analyst. The PI® report provides you with a brief overview of the results of the Predictive Index® and prompts you to consider many aspects of the results not contained in the overview. If you have not yet attended the Predictive Index Management Workshop™, please consult someone who has attended in order to complete the report.

STRONGEST BEHAVIORS

Rhian will most strongly express the following behaviors:

- Proactively connects quickly to others; she's open and sharing of herself. Builds and leverages relationships to get work done.
- Comfortably fluent and fast talk, in volume. She enthusiastically persuades and motivates others by considering their point of view and adjusting her delivery.
- Collaborative; usually works with and through others. Intuitive understanding of team cohesion, dynamics, and interpersonal relations.
- Socially focused, she generally empathizes with people, seeing their point of view or understanding their emotions. Positive communication.
- Teaches and shares; she's generally interested in working collaboratively with others to help out.
- Friendly and service-oriented; she drives for the 'greater good' rather than her own goals. Promotes teamwork by sharing authority.

SUMMARY

Rhian is unassuming, unselfish, and has a sincere and genuine interest in other people and a strong, intuitive understanding of them. Outgoing and friendly, she enjoys working with people and is lively, pleasant company.

A warm and friendly communicator, Rhian is able to stimulate and motivate others while being aware of and responsive to their needs and concerns. Her outgoing personality and sincere, interested attitude make her easily accessible, and she gets along well with a wide variety of people.

Her drive is altruistic, directed at working with and for others: for the team, for customers and for the company. A cooperative, willing worker, Rhian can be particularly effective as a teacher or trainer, communicating the company's policies, programs, and systems with enthusiasm and spirit.

Working at a faster-than-average pace, she learns quickly. More concerned with effective communication than she is with detail in depth, she is about average in her level of accuracy in handling details and too impatient to work with details as repetitive routine. She communicates flexibly, adjusting her style for different people, and is generally most effective when discussing intangibles such as ideas, feelings, or visions.

If her job permits, she will delegate details and responsibility and will follow up in a friendly, supportive manner to assure that work gets done on time. She has an active interest in the development of people for the company's benefit and will encourage such development in her subordinates.

In general, Rhian is a cooperative teamworker who respects company authority and policies, which she will accept and communicate enthusiastically.

MANAGEMENT STYLE

As a manager of people or projects, Rhian will be:

- Focused on building and cultivating a productive, harmonious team
- Comfortable delegating both authority and details; her follow-up will be in a friendly, supportive manner assuring that work gets done on-time and generally within company policy
- Warm and persuasive; she manages by walking around, gathering input from others and using verbal encouragement and enthusiasm to gain support
- Cautious in situations which obviously break from company policy; will build consensus before making exceptions
- Actively interested in the development of people for the company's benefit and will encourage such development of her employees; personally teaches and shares
- A willing team member and participant, even of teams that she manages.

INFLUENCING STYLE

As an influencer, Rhian will be:

- Friendly and approachable, communicating very well with many different styles

- Focused on understanding others – who they are, what their likes/dislikes are, how they fit in with the other players in the organization
- Skillful with the emotional aspects of influencing others; connecting with others and leveraging the relationship to gain agreement
- Flexible and service-oriented, she will read others' needs well and ensure their satisfaction; eager to find a mutually beneficial solution
- Adept at conveying how the idea or concept will help others; somewhat less concerned with the technical specifications of how it works
- Generally liked and trusted by others in repeated contact; adept at maintaining and growing productive business relationships.

MANAGEMENT STRATEGIES

To maximize her effectiveness, productivity, and job satisfaction, consider providing Rhian with the following:

- Opportunities to work in frequent contact with other people
- Supportive, encouraging, and collaborative managers, peers, and/or trusted advisors
- Clear, specific description of her job and responsibilities, and of company policies and goals Assurance of security and recognition in social and status terms.

Prepared by Roy Lance Japor on 12/22/2013

Once all the data is gathered, including interviews, personality assessments and so on, the employees' information (Hi-Po and non-Hi-Po) is plotted on what is referred to as a "9-Box" grid. The example below depicts a typical organization's 9-Box grid. The x-axis represents Performance (based on like merit reviews and other key indicators) and the y-axis shows Potential (based on the personality assessment, 360 feedback, and so on). Ideally, an organization's future leaders will be in the upper right quadrant of the grid (i.e. High Performance and High Potential)

	Low	Moderate	High
High	"Rough Diamond" Low Performer/ High Potential	"Future Star" Moderate Performer/High Potential	"Consistent Star" High Performer/High Potential
Moderate	"Inconsistent Player" Low Performer/Moderate Potential	"Key Player" Moderate Performer/ Moderate Potential	"Current Star" High Performer/Moderate Potential
Low	"Talent Risk" Low Performer/Low Potential	"Solid Professional" Moderate Performer/Low Potential	"High Professional" High Performer/Low Potential

Potential Assessment (y-axis)

Performance Assessment (x-axis)

The Challenge of Succession Planning

In the large organization that I worked with, it was taboo to share the names of employees who were listed as HI-POs. Why, you may ask? Well, for a few reasons. Some leaders thought this information might make the Hi-PO employees ask for bigger, unbudgeted merit increases. Some felt that sharing this information could be frustrating for Hi-POs if the position did not become vacant fast enough for them to take on a new role. Others thought the information could serve as a demotivator for other 'non-Hi-PO' team members!

Over my years with this organization, I met with several high potential employees as they made the decision to leave the company. The exit interviews all yielded the same information: the employee knew they did great work, but did not have any awareness that they were being prepared to be future leaders. Remember what I shared earlier in this book? A key human need is the need for growth. These employees knew that they were ready for the next step and hoped the organization would provide them with a roadmap to help achieve that goal.

My recommendation is to be transparent with your succession plan. Your best employees need to know that you see them as valuable. Once you let the employee know that she is a high potential employee, work with them on a plan for their future success. Show them that you are invested in their success.

Note on Low Performance/Low Potential: The succession planning process will also cast a spotlight on your low performers with low potential. Don't be afraid to take action. Ensuring Maximum Employee engagement means creating a culture that supports high performance and does not mean casting a blind eye to bad performance with the hope of retaining as many people as possible. Believe me, your employees already know who the poor performers in the company are. When you do take action, be sure to be tactful and respectful. Empathy goes a long way when communicating with employees who are not meeting the organizational standards.

CHAPTER 11:
How Your Management Style Can Impact Maximum Employee Engagement

"If you wait long enough, difficult people either quit, retire or die. That's my management style."

If you are a GenXer or Baby boomer, you may recall the traditional role of a manager. In fact, many TV sitcoms poke fun at these stereotypes. Managers, mostly male, were seen sitting in their offices while barking out orders. That style of managing is not conducive to today's employees and to maximum employee engagement.

As we discussed earlier, employment is PERSONAL. As a manager, you have a great deal of influence over the level of engagement of your teams. Your management style is the key to having employees that have achieved maximum engagement. It is therefore very important for leaders to pay close attention to their management style and the impact it has on the people they lead.

In a 2010 Harvard Business Review, Liz Wiseman and Greg McKeown identified two types of managers and their impact on the performance and level of employee engagement. (www.sharpmedicalrecruiting/download)

Wiseman and McKeown refer to the first group as "Diminishers." Diminishers tend to be the types of leader who hoard information, creates a tense environment, and make abrupt centralized decisions that confuse employees. We all have met a Diminisher or two in our time. I recall working with one organization where turnover in the executive ranks was extremely high. In fact, one of their locations had over thirteen leaders in less than 10 years! Can you imagine the loss of productivity and skilled talent? With each new leader the mission, vision, and values changed. It was difficult to attain maximum engagement with so much leadership change. Exit interviews with the leaders all resulted in the same feedback: the employees felt that the goals of their manager kept changing, which resulted in the belief that they were in an environment designed for their failure. In addition, several of the leaders shared that they felt they were treated more like children than professional adults.

The Diminisher style will clearly diminish your employee population, as your best employees will leave to join organizations where they feel respected and valued.

The second management style observed by Wiseman and McKeown is termed "Multipliers." In stark contrast to the Diminisher style, these managers attract talented people and use them to their full potential. They create a challenging yet creative environment for people to think critically and encourage a culture of debate to find the best ideas. Multiplier managers are not afraid to share information, as they are not concerned about employees 'stealing' their jobs. The Multipliers believe that their success comes from supporting and developing the people on their teams.

To ensure maximum employee engagement managers, you need to project the Multiplier style of management. This style will show your people that you are invested in their success above your own.

THE FIVE TYPES OF MULTIPLIERS AND DIMINISHERS

Diminishers	Multipliers
The Empire Builder: Hoards resources and underutilizes talent	**The Talent Magnet**: Attracts talented people and uses them to their highest potential
The Tyrant: Creates a tense environment that suppresses people's thinking and capabilities	**The Liberator**: Creates an intense environment that requires people's best thinking and work
The Know-It-All: Gives directives that demonstrate how much he or she knows	**The Challenger**: Defines an opportunity that causes people to stretch their thinking and behaviors
The Decision Maker: Makes centralized, abrupt decisions that confuse the organization	**The Debate Maker**: Drives sound decisions by cultivating rigorous debate among team members
The Micro-Manager: Drives results through his or her personal involvement	**The Investor**: Gives other people ownership of results and invests in their success

BE A MULTIPLIER MANAGER TO GAIN MAXIMUM EMPLOYEE ENGAGEMENT!

Final Thoughts

Maximum Employee Engagement is not about tenure; it's not about keeping your employees with you all the way to their retirement (though that would be nice if it happens). The days of employees staying with one organization throughout their entire working life are over. In fact, research has shown that today's employees have an average tenure of three years.

The goal of Maximum Employee Engagement, therefore, is to ensure that during the employee's tenure with your company, you ensure maximum productivity through consistently meeting the employees' human needs and to create a level of 'discipleship' within your employee population, you retain.

To achieve maximum employee engagement, employees need to believe in the vision, mission, and values of the organization and continue to do so even after they leave your organization in three years. If this is accomplished, when these employees encounter others in their social network, they will help you to attract new employees who will also attain *Maximum Employee Engagement.*

ABOUT THE AUTHOR

Rhian Sharp is the founder and CEO of Sharp Medical Recruiting and Consulting. Rhian has been an HR Leader for almost 20 years and a Healthcare leader for over 16 years (working with industry leading companies like McKesson and Gentiva). In 2009 Rhian was named the first HR Director for the newly created state agency DBHDD the agency consisted of the 7 behavioral health hospitals in the state of Georgia.

Rhian is a true 'go getter'. She earned a BA in Economics from Georgia State University and her MBA and Masters Certificate in Human Resources. She is an avid fitness enthusiast having run over 16 half marathons and competing in fitness challenge.

Rhian brings this same energy and determination into her business. Rhian's roots in the healthcare industry go back a generation. Her mother was a registered nurse from the twin island republic of Trinidad and Tobago. As a young child Rhian spent many summer holidays visiting her mother's clinic.

Rhian is passionate about driving businesses forward with the right people. She is skilled at high volume recruiting, medical direct placement and executive searches. She is viewed by many as a trusted Advisor, mentor and coach.

She can be reached at Rhian@SharpMedicalRecruiting.com

For helpful tips and useful templates to improve your employee engagement, go to: www.SharpMedicalRecruiting.com/MEE

YOUR PURCHASE HELPS A WORTHY CAUSE

A PORTION OF THE PROCEEDS FROM THE SALE OF THIS BOOK WILL GO TO OUR CHARITY. MEDICAL TEAMS INTERNATIONAL.

About Medical Teams International

We see human suffering as a call — not just to open our hearts, but to move our feet. We are compelled by our Christian faith into action — a team, guided by compassion and magnified by expertise.

We respond to disasters around the world—and here at home—by sending teams of volunteer medical professionals and medical supplies to care for the sick and injured. We also mobilize long-term health improvement programs, collaborating with established partners within each community to ensure that our work has a sustainable impact.

Medical Teams International provides medical and dental care, humanitarian aid, and holistic development programs to all people in need, regardless of religion, nationality, sex, or race.

Values: Who We Are

- **We are courageous.** We are bold and we know it takes bravery to break down barriers and do what we do.

- **We are tenacious.** We have that can-do spirit. We don't give up when the going gets tough.

- **We are accountable.** We take our responsibilities and roles seriously. We have integrity in all we do.

- **We are selfless.** We put others before ourselves. Always. That is who we are.

- **We are not alone.** We know God is always with us as we stand in solidarity with others.

Countries served by Medical Teams International

http://www.MedicalTeams.org

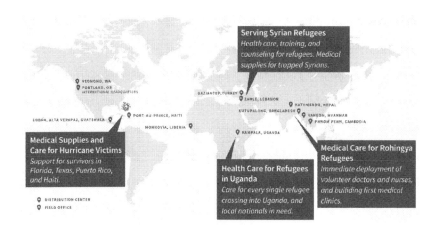

Made in the USA
Columbia, SC
29 April 2018